Good Habit Book

A Rhyming Adventure

The Reading Reindeer Book

Title: Good Habit Book : A Rhyming Adventure

Published By:
Print N Prose Private Limited
Website: printnprosebooks.com
email: contact@printnprosebooks.com

Publisher's Address: 433, Ground Floor, A Block,
Sector 47, Noida, 201301, Uttar Pradesh
Phone: +91-120-4312018

Edition Details: First Edition
ISBN: 978-81-964573-4-1
Copyright © 2023 PRINT N PROSE PRIVATE LIMITED

Author : Niti Shukla

ALL RIGHTS RESERVED. No part of this book may be reproduced or transmitted in any form by any means, electronic or physical, including photocopying and recording, or by any information storage and retrieval system, except as may be expressly permitted in writing by the publisher.

INDEX

1. Sleep on time..5
2. Wake up early in morning........................6
3. Make your bed..7
4. Brush Teeth daily...8
5. Bath daily...9
6. Wash your hands..10
7. Drink water..11
8. Eat healthy..12
9. Use tissue...13
10. Sit properly...14
11. Eat properly..15
12. Finish your meal...16
13. Use Table & Chair.....................................17
14. Read Books...18
15. Do your homework daily........................19
16. Reach school on time..............................20
17. Be creative..21
18. Follow Time Table.....................................22
19. Play with friends..23
20. Teamwork..24
21. Play mind games.......................................25
22. Share your food...26
23. Share Toys..27
24. Go to park..28
25. Exercise daily..29

INDEX

26. Use Stairs..30
27. Practice Yoga..31
28. Explore Nature..32
29. Pray to God..33
30. Say Thank you..34
31. Say Sorry...35
32. Respect elders...36
33. Spend time with grandparents.................37
34. Help your parents....................................38
35. Be kind to others.....................................39
36. Take care of your pets.............................40
37. Feed birds...41
38. Plant Trees..42
39. Keep your room clean..............................43
40. Wear clean cloths....................................44
41. Use trash bin...45
42. Recycle waste...46
43. Save money...47
44. Wait for your turn....................................48
45. Use marked crossway..............................49
46. Say no to junk food.................................50
47. Don't doodle on the walls.......................51
48. Don't be greedy......................................52
49. Don't use bad language..........................53
50. Make friends and never fight..................54

SLEEP ON TIME

Close your eyes, it's time to rest,
Sleeping on time, you'll feel your best!

WAKE UP EARLY IN MORNING

When the sun starts to rise and the day is new,
Wake up early, there's so much to do!

MAKE YOUR BED

Start the day with a tidy space,
Make your bed, a neat embrace!

BRUSH TEETH DAILY

Brush your little teeth, shining bright,
Every day, morning and night!

BATH DAILY

Splash in the water, bubbles all around,
Take a daily bath, freshness can be found!

WASH YOUR HANDS

Before you eat or after play,
Wash your hands, keep germs away

DRINK WATER

Water is clear, pure and true,
Drink it up, it's healthy for you!

EAT HEALTHY

Veggies and fruits, colorful and bright,
Eat healthy food, grow strong and right.

USE TISSUE

Cough or sneeze, use a tissue with care,
Keep germs away, show others you care!

SIT PROPERLY

Sit up straight, tall and strong,
Proper posture helps us all day long!

EAT PROPERLY

Take small bites, chew them well,
Eating properly, our bodies can excel!

FINISH YOUR MEAL

Empty your plate, no food should go to waste,
Finish your meal with a happy, healthy taste.

USE TABLE & CHAIR

Sit at your table, chair just right,
Ready to study, with all your might!

READ BOOKS

Books are treasures, full of delight,
Read them with joy, day or night!

DO YOUR HOMEWORK DAILY

Sit down and learn, pencil in hand,
Do your homework, knowledge expands!

REACH SCHOOL ON TIME

Hurry to school, don't be late,
Arrive on time, learning can't wait.

BE CREATIVE

Paint with colors, let your imagination soar,
Make creative masterpieces, forevermore!

FOLLOW TIME TABLE

Time table helps us stay on track,
Follow it well, and never look back!

PLAY WITH FRIENDS

Together we play, hand in hand,
Friends bring joy, a magical band!

TEAM WORK

Together we work, hand in hand,
Teamwork makes us strong and grand!

PLAY MIND GAMES

Puzzles and riddles, games of the mind,
Playing mind games, fun we will find!

SHARE YOUR FOOD

Sharing is caring, it's a special treat,
Share your food, make someone's day sweet!

SHARE TOYS

Sharing is caring, it's so much fun,
Play together, everyone gets a turn.

GO TO PARK

Run and play in the park so green,
Exploring and learning, a joyful scene!

EXERCISE DAILY

Jump, run, and play with delight,
Exercise daily, it feels just right!

USE STAIRS

Step by step, we climb with care,
Using stairs keeps us fit and aware!

PRACTICE YOGA

Stretch and breathe, find your inner calm,
Practicing yoga, like a peaceful charm!

EXPLORE NATURE

Step outside, explore with glee,
Nature's wonders, for us to see

PRAY TO GOD

Fold your hands and bow your head,
Praying to God, our hearts are led.

SAY THANK YOU

When someone is kind, don't forget to say, "Thank you!" It brightens their day.

SAY SORRY

When we make a mistake, let's make it right,
Say "I'm sorry" with a heart so bright!

RESPECT ELDERS

Listen to elders, wise and kind,
Obeying them brings joy you'll find!

SPEND TIME WITH GRANDPARENTS

Laugh and play, stories to unfold,
With grandparents dear, memories of gold!

HELP YOUR PARENTS

Helping parents is a wonderful way,
To make them smile, each and every day!

BE KIND TO OTHERS

Share a smile, lend a hand,
Being kind to others, let love expand!

TAKE CARE OF YOUR PETS

Feed them well, give them love and care,
Pets are family, treat them fair!

FEED BIRDS

Spread some seeds, watch them fly,
Feed the birds, way up high!

PLANT TREES

Dig a hole, plant a tree,
Watch it grow, happy and free!

KEEP YOUR ROOM CLEAN

Toys in their place, no mess to be seen,
A clean room, a happy and tidy routine!

WEAR CLEAN CLOTHS

Wear clean clothes, fresh and neat,
Looking smart from head to feet.

USE TRASH BIN

Keep our earth clean, don't make a mess,
Use the trash bin, it's the best!

RECYCLE WASTE

Recycle waste, give it a new start,
Helping the Earth, playing our part!

SAVE MONEY

Save your coins, drop them in,
Piggy bank smiles, as savings begin!

WAIT FOR YOUR TURN

In line we stand, patient and calm,
Waiting our turn, with a happy charm.

USE MARKED CROSSWAY

At the marked crossway, we stop and wait,
Safety first, no need to hesitate!

SAY NO TO JUNK FOOD

Choose fruits and veggies, healthy and true,
Say no to junk food, your body will thank you!

DON'T DOODLE ON WALLS

Crayons on paper, colors so bright,
Don't doodle on walls, keep them clean and white!

DON'T BE GREEDY

Share and care, don't be greedy,
In kindness and generosity, find your beauty.

DON'T USE BAD LANGUAGE

Use words that are kind, gentle, and nice,
No bad language, let's keep it wise!

MAKE FRIENDS AND NEVER FIGHT

Hands are for helping, not for a fight,
Spread peace and love, shining bright!

www.ingramcontent.com/pod-product-compliance
Lightning Source LLC
LaVergne TN
LVHW070207080526
838202LV00063B/6569